TREEFROGS

DOUG WECHSLER
THE ACADEMY OF NATURAL SCIENCES

The Rosen Publishing Group's
PowerKids Press™
New York

For Ron Hirschi, a great guy and an inspiration to me

About the Author
Wildlife biologist, ornithologist, and photographer Doug Wechsler has studied birds, snakes, frogs, and other wildlife around the world. Doug Wechsler works at The Academy of Natural Sciences of Philadelphia, a natural history museum. As part of his job, he travels to rain forests and remote parts of the world to take pictures of birds. He has taken part in expeditions to Ecuador, the Philippines, Borneo, Cuba, Cameroon, and many other countries.

Published in 2002 by The Rosen Publishing Group, Inc.
29 East 21st Street, New York, NY 10010

First Edition

Book Design: Michael de Guzman, Emily Muschinske

Project Editor: Kathy Campbell

Photo Credits: All photographs © Doug Wechsler
pp. 4, 7, and 19 red-eyed treefrog (*Agalychnis callidryas*); p. 11 (inset) harlequin treefrog (*Rhacophorus pardalis*); treefrog (no common name) (*Leptopelis* sp.); p. 12 pepper treefrog or veined treefrog (*Phrynohyas venulosa*); p. 12 (inset) pine barrens treefrog (*Hyla andersoni*); p. 15 hourglass treefrog (*Hyla ebraccata*); p. 16 masked treefrog (*Smilisca phaeota*); p. 20 common gray treefrog (*Hyla versicolor*); p. 8 Cuban treefrog (*Osteopilus septentrionalis*); p. 22 spotted treefrog (*Hyla punctata*).

Wechsler, Doug.
Treefrogs / Doug Wechsler.
    p. cm. — (The Really wild life of frogs)
  ISBN 0-8239-5859-0 (lib. bdg.)
1. Hylidae—Juvenile literature. [1. Tree frogs. 2. Frogs.] I. Title.
  QL668.E24 W425 2002
  597.8'78—dc21
                                                                        2001000605

Manufactured in the United States of America

CONTENTS

TREEFROGS AROUND THE WORLD

Treefrogs come in many shapes, sizes, and colors. They are yellow, green, red, and brown. They are like jewels in a tropical forest. They might also live in your backyard.

Treefrogs are climbing frogs. They have special toe pads that let them cling to leaves, twigs, and tree trunks. Most treefrogs are small. Some treefrogs are less than 1 inch (25 mm) long. The largest treefrog grows to more than 5 ½ inches (140 mm) long. Treefrogs live in many parts of the world. The only places you will not find them are deserts and areas that are very cold for most of the year. There are more than 900 treefrog **species** in the world. About 26 species live in North America.

Red-eyed treefrogs live in the forests of Central America. More kinds of treefrogs live in Central and South America than anywhere else.

TOE PADS, TICKET TO THE TREES

What put the tree into treefrog? Toe pads did. Toe pads allow treefrogs to climb. Toe pads are large, rounded tips on the treefrog's toes. The pads make it possible for treefrogs to cling to branches, leaves, or even glass. When a treefrog jumps onto a leaf, the toe pads keep the treefrog from falling off.

Toe pads are moist. The moisture allows them to cling to smooth surfaces. The moisture on toe pads is not sticky like glue. It is mostly water. Water can hold things together on its own. To see how this works, cut two small squares from a plastic bag. Place one on top of the other with a drop of water in between. The water makes them stick together.

The toe pads on the underside of a treefrog's foot (shown in the inset picture) help it to jump from leaf to leaf without falling.

DOUG SAYS

HANDLING RED-EYED TREEFROGS MAKES SOME PEOPLE SNEEZE.

COLOR CHANGE

Treefrogs can quickly change the tone of their skin from light to dark. Warmth and light backgrounds can make them turn light. Cold and dark backgrounds can make them turn dark.

A few treefrogs can change colors. Gray treefrogs can turn from gray to green to blend in with leaves. The lemur treefrog can turn from a reddish color to green. Barking treefrogs can change from plain, bright green to green with dark spots.

Most treefrogs are colored for **camouflage**. Their patterns and colors help them blend in with **lichens**, stones, leaves, or bark. The camouflage keeps them safe from birds and other **predators** that hunt by sight.

Some treefrogs look like the bark on which they rest. The Cuban treefrog uses camouflage to keep it safe while sleeping.

Treefrogs have big eyes to help them see better at night. Treefrogs are nocturnal, which means they are active at night. They find their **prey** by sight. They also make giant leaps from one twig to another. It takes a good eye to land safely.

Big eyes can open wide to let in a lot of light. Large eyes also mean big **retinas**. The retina is in the back of the eye. It senses light and sends messages to the brain. A big retina helps a frog see in low light. The colored part of a treefrog's eyes is called the **iris**. It opens wide in the dark of night to let in more light. It closes to a slit during the day to protect the eye from too much light.

Large eyes help treefrogs to see at night when they are most active.

A TRILL, A HONK, AND A GROSS SOUND

Every species of treefrog has its own call. Gray treefrogs **trill** in May and June. **Pine barrens** treefrogs honk about once each second. The pepper treefrog makes a kind of sound we try not to make in public.

To sing its song, a treefrog fills its lungs with air. It pushes the air through its **vocal cords** into a pouch next to its mouth. The air shakes the vocal cords to make the sound. The pouch helps to spread those sounds into the air. It also saves the air to recycle it. The air goes back into the lungs and the frog is ready to call again.

Only male treefrogs make loud calls. Their songs tell females, "Come here to mate." They also tell other males, "This is my spot, stay away!" CALUMET CITY PUBLIC LIBRARY

Pepper treefrogs (left) and pine barrens treefrogs (right) each have their own special call. Barking treefrogs have two different calls. They bark from the treetops and "wonk" in water.

EGGS IN THE TREES

Each species of treefrog has its own way to lay eggs. Treefrogs usually lay eggs in small ponds or creeks. Often these ponds hold water for only part of the year. In Borneo, an island in the South China Sea, rhinoceros mud **wallows** make good **breeding** ponds for treefrogs. Sadly, rhinoceroses have been over-hunted there. As the rhinoceroses disappear, what will happen to the frogs?

In tropical forests, some treefrogs lay their eggs on leaves above the water. When the tadpoles wriggle out of the eggs, they fall into the stream. Other treefrogs use knotholes high in trees. These treefrogs spend their whole lives in the forest **canopy**.

Most treefrogs lay their eggs in water. The hourglass treefrog lays its eggs on grass just above a pond.

DOUG SAYS

I SAW MASKED TREEFROG EGGS IN A MUDDY FOOTPRINT FILLED WITH WATER IN COSTA RICA.

DOUG SAYS

I FOUND CUBAN TREEFROGS BREEDING IN WATER THAT COLLECTED IN AN UPSIDE-DOWN CAR.

TADPOLES

Tadpoles are eating machines. Their job is to grow quickly. Tadpoles eat rotting vegetation, **bacteria**, and **algae**. In North America, most treefrogs spend from 6 to 10 weeks as tadpoles before they become frogs.

Many treefrog tadpoles scrape algae off plants or dead leaves in water. Some eat other tadpoles. A few rain forest treefrog tadpoles live in plants that hold water. They eat frog eggs laid in the water.

Fish are a tadpole's number-one enemy. For this reason, many treefrogs lay their eggs where there are no fish. These places can be puddles, knotholes in trees, or seasonal ponds that hold water for only part of the year.

Masked treefrog tadpoles feed on rotten fruit in a mud puddle.

WHY WE LOVE RED-EYED TREEFROGS

Recently the red-eyed treefrog has become a symbol of the tropical forest. Why do we love the red-eyed treefrog so much? The big eyes and the smile make it look happy, which makes us happy. Its red, green, blue, and yellow colors are cheery. Its bright red eyes catch our attention.

This frog looks very unusual and **exotic**. It is a reminder of all the unusual forms of life that live in tropical forests. Not every animal in the jungle looks so cheery, but each one is important. Tropical forests are important to us for many reasons. They help to keep the land from becoming a desert. They provide us with medicines. They are the home of the treefrog.

Colorful red-eyed treefrogs always get attention. When resting, they close their eyes and hide their bright sides with their legs.

HOLD THAT WATER

Treefrogs spend most of their time out of water. The soft skin of **amphibians** lets water enter and escape quickly. Frogs can shape their bodies to keep in as much water as possible. When a treefrog is resting, it pulls its legs and arms up against its body. It flattens its whole body against tree bark or leaves. This reduces the amount of skin in contact with the dry air.

Treefrogs usually seek moist or shady places to rest. Some rest beneath peeling bark, in tree hollows, or on plants that trap water in their leaves. A treefrog's skin makes a type of slime, which keeps it from drying out. The bumpy skin of a treefrog's belly soaks up water quickly, just like a bumpy paper towel.

This gray treefrog has its arms and legs pulled tight against its body to hold in moisture while it rests.

ODD TREEFROGS

Most treefrogs are similar in looks and habits, but there are a few strange species. One treefrog has horns in the back of its head and carries its eggs on its back. Another group of treefrogs, called **marsupial** frogs, carries the eggs and tadpoles in a pouch in the back. In some marsupial frogs, the tadpoles turn into frogs while they are still inside the egg. They hatch right after turning into frogs and then leave the pouch.

In the rain forests of Southeast Asia and South America, there are treefrogs that can glide. Flying treefrogs have large **webs** between their fingers and toes. When they jump, they spread their toes wide and drift down through the air.

GLOSSARY

algae (AL-jee) Plants without roots or stems that usually live in the water.

amphibians (am-FIH-bee-unz) Animals that can live on land and in the water.

bacteria (bak-TEER-ee-uh) Tiny living things that can only be seen with a microscope and that sometimes cause illness or decay.

breeding (BREED-ing) Getting together to mate and lay eggs or have babies.

camouflage (KA-muh-flahj) The color or pattern of an animal's feathers, fur, or skin that helps it blend into its surroundings.

canopy (CA-nuh-pee) The treetop level in a forest.

exotic (ek-ZAH-tik) Something that comes from another country or is strange.

iris (EYE-ris) The round muscle in the eye that is colored and surrounds the pupil.

lichens (LY-kenz) Forms of life made up of a fungus and an alga growing together.

marsupial (mar-SOO-pee-ul) A type of mammal in which the mother carries the young in its pouch.

pine barrens (PYN BAR-ens) Open woods of pine trees growing on sandy soil.

predators (PREH-duh-ters) Animals that kill other animals for food.

prey (PRAY)   An animal that is eaten by another animal for food.

retinas (REH-tin-ahz) The innermost layers of the eyes that are sensitive to light.

species (SPEE-sheez) A single kind of plant or animal. For example, all people are one species.

trill (TRIL) A rapidly repeating musical note.

vocal cords (VOH-kul KORDZ) Thin strands in the voice box that make sound when air rushes through them.

wallows (WAH-lohz) Wet, muddy places made by animals that like mud baths.

webs (WEBZ) The skin between the toes of ducks, frogs, and other animals that swim.

INDEX

WEB SITES

To learn more about treefrogs, check out these Web sites:

www.belizezoo.org/zoo/zoo/herps/fro/fro1.html
www.loscan.com/gafrogs/Docs/pine.barrens.tfrog.html
www.npwrc.usgs.gov/narcam/idguide/hcinerea.htm